In a Mist

Also by Geoffrey O'Brien

POETRY

A Book of Maps
The Hudson Mystery
Floating City: Selected Poems 1978-1995
A View of Buildings and Water
Red Sky Café
Early Autumn

PROSE

Hardboiled America: Lurid Paperbacks and the Masters of Noir
Dream Time: Chapters from the Sixties
The Phantom Empire
The Times Square Story
Bardic Deadlines: Reviewing Poetry 1984-95
The Browser's Ecstasy: A Meditation on Reading
Castaways of the Image Planet: Movies, Show Business, Public Spectacle
Sonata for Jukebox: An Autobiography of My Ears
The Fall of the House of Walworth
Stolen Glimpses, Captive Shadows: Writing on Film 2002-2012

Geoffrey O'Brien

In a Mist

Shearsman Books

First published in the United Kingdom in 2015 by
Shearsman Books
50 Westons Hill Drive
Emersons Green
BRISTOL
BS16 7DF

Shearsman Books Ltd Registered Office
30–31 St. James Place, Mangotsfield, Bristol BS16 9JB
(this address not for correspondence)

www.shearsman.com

ISBN 978-1-84861-360-7

ACKNOWLEDGEMENTS
Some of these poems appeared originally in *The Baffler,
Battersea Review, Black Clock, Hambone, Jacket, Little Star,
New American Writing, Notre Dame Review,* and *Projector.*

Contents

To Flaminia

I

In Memory of Oppen

"The solitary are obsessed"

1

a plain kitchen
table, his face
tilted downward

with eyes closed
as if to listen in
on what he would say next –

"insufficient care
for the meaning of words" –
painful to think so –

or, of prepositions
"they're hell on wheels" –
waterfront apartments

emptied of everything
but what they did not
in the first place contain –

to inhabit
a continual erosion
of what is there

2

not that he did
not want to speak
the words aloud

but it made him
uneasy – to mistake
happenstance for the real,

if the heart should startle
at a tone of voice –
special pleading –

preferred
to remove himself
from the utterance,

a weathered
free-standing hulk
taking its own place

3

to wake up
in the middle
of a chilly afternoon

to the presence
of words – hull,
pavements, gull –

a gray world
saved
in time for autumn,

the stairwell
winding down
toward late light –

empty, flat,
alien – a generation
fills the air

with their living absence
in each worn handle,
each cracked brick –

ghost words –
more solid
than anything –

come carrying
fifty years
into the stone yard

4

all that time
they had been in apartments
and cars,

the sun had moved
across the room,
night dropped down,

a foot touched
the bare floor –
key grinding in lock –

under a spell
until it said so:
wake –

when you get back
to where you were
before you were going there –

to find a postcard
undelivered – "man,
read this book"

April

for Robert O'Brien (1941-2009)

1

There was a driveway
In afternoon light
Behind blinds

I did not know where,
Or if that was light
Of California or Chicago,

Only that I wanted
To be anywhere else

2

I could not bear
To have him see
I could not bear

To see
He could not bear
To see

3

Head flung back
Neck twisted sideways
Jaw tilted agape

The eyes rolled up
In their sockets
In astonishment

You are already stone
And will soon
Be flame

4

"Everything palpitates
And I begin to live"

The song of Lakmé
The immortal soprano

Condemned to flames
In tropical green stage setting

5

There was a world
In which everything was horrible

Faces turned away
Forever in hatred or disgust

Like the political radio
Murmuring poison

In the unattended
Hospice room

Doing the opposite
Of what the Virgin does

When she pleads for souls

6

Skull
Now untuned

Scraped of its images
Of leeches

Or famished soldiers
On scorched plain –

No fanfare
Or enumerated droplet of music

Most alive
When it pretends to die

Like Petrouchka,
Or Nevsky's warriors

That a mezzo
Searches for by torchlight

7

If I were to translate
This poem into
Your language,

The only
You were fluent in,
It would have to say

"Mahler Ravel
Puccini Britten
Sullivan Gershwin

Copland Bernstein
Bach Hindemith
Weill Strauss Stravinsky

Debussy Verdi
Poulenc Walton Orff
Prokofiev Wagner"

8

It all exists
In time

Except
For music

In which
Time exists

9

The glance
Does not persist

Beyond those
Who exchange it

And if they do not exchange it

Has not even the chance
Not to persist

For S.

"and thereupon the spirit faded and was gone"

Forty years
since you stepped
into nothing
the subway roars
as if still
hungry for you.

...

What stays
is heavy.
What was light
went.

...

In your place
a sort of spectral
confetti
of hospital visit,
wake seen
from boat's rail,
pills in a hat-band,
dragon scroll, a closet
soft with overcoats.

...

Watery icon
of a smile
turning into a laugh,
a laugh into a kiss
that flares out, the bulb
switched off in haste.

...

Scraps of voice
and eye-glint by now
too faint to recognize,
like a line
on a discarded
piece of paper –
"the boat in the drowned park"
(a phrase to attract
your eye a moment)
or "I dreamt the bus
wouldn't stop" –
something that
looked like poetry,
to crawl inside
and zip the tent after.

...

Undivided days
of closed drapes
and Viennese dissonance,
unending board game,
an offering-plate
of picture cards,
pond, smoke,
cloud, rope,
lamp, chalk,
doll tied down
in a chair, given drugs
while music played –
wait, I haven't
finished – days,
days of drapes –
already said that –
only so that daylight
be lassoed to hold steady.

...

Don't fall down,
don't step into death
as into a novel
you always meant to read,
long and dark
and Russian,
that when opened
is a smear
of erasure.

...

Came breeze howling
down back stairs
toward the park,
at midnight already,
having dozed,
and Bobby Vee
lost in Scopitone
sang "night
has a thousand
eyes" – no,
you had already split,
even before you went.

...

An invention of dawn,
the overturning water jar,
ballet lesson for ghosts –
and stashed under a pillow
in the dance studio
your stained copy
of "Symbolism An Introduction"
heavily underscored
in waterproof pink.

...

At forty years distance
anything louder
would by now
have scared you off.

A wisp is too harsh.
At mere hint of sight
all parts of you
drop into the glare.

An Averted Face

1

"The sorrow that has come out
in your eyes, looking down,
or in your lips, tight-pressed
as if never to say something,
that sorrow you feel shame for,
and for lips and eyes
impatient to announce
where you bid be silent
or show, where you say
shut, hold back."

2

The book where I hid the poem
was meant for no one's eyes,
least of all yours, even if,
reading it forty years after,
I just glimpse your face
turning away angry
or disappointed into the unseeable,
only long enough to wonder
whose shame was written there,
or whose sorrow or silence.

Another One for Joel

This is not the poem,
this is just the place
where the poem disappears –

droplets of time
disgorged out of the visible
dry up in the new light,
the anti-light –

glisten as they pop
into the transparence
where the images go,
mess of things seen, the crawl
between hedges,
stone bench in desert, patterns
of silvery glitter
smeared across a blank wall –

it takes everything with it
when it goes – the solutions
dissolve in themselves.

II

David Goodis

His room had a bed,
a table and a chair.

He turned and looked around the room
and tried to see something.

The quiet became very thick
and it pressed against him.

The heat
was stronger than any liquor.

He told himself to relax
and play it cool.

He told himself
to get back on balance.

As he went out of the house
he could still hear the screaming.

And later, turning the street corners,
he didn't bother to look at the street signs.

Monsieur Zero

1. The Lost One

He fell into being
a fool, he found
odd-shaped stones
that depicted his luck
and walked
where was no shade
for sun glare
until forgetting his name
he puzzled a way back
to his home streets,
muttering so no one
could hear, Where
is my name, I have
lost my name, and fear
I shall never find it.

2. Working Life: The End of the Week

…The main suite crowded
as always – signs of rain
on the roof terrace – in a corner
a girl is bending forward
to write something (a phone number?)
on her foot, her instep – how curious –
and I have my stack of magazines

to hand out at the conference – I'm feeling
social, eager to get involved with people
by smiling at them – at every point
along the corridor co-workers
are murmuring, kidding around, yawning,
consulting – it would all be fine
if dusk didn't come, if everybody
didn't finally drift toward the bus stop…

3. To the Body Tangled in Dust

I didn't know dust could tangle
until for most of a year
the room went unswept
where someone looked into the dark
to scrape through its layers
to the other sky –
Past unhealed gouges
with dirt in them –
To the music of chopped-off
retorts: "Didn't you,
almost, so it's thin under it?" –
Stray hisses layered like mica –
There where everything
happens to the body,
or in it,
or in its presence.

Memoir of a Sheltered Life

1
Decades later
he went back to the island

looking for scraps
of a marooned life

to find only logbook entries
with every other line eaten away.

2
For fear the sun might explode
he stayed home in his attic

drawing small diagrams
of foreign ports.

3
As if no one had ever
told him anything,
or he hadn't listened.

As if he had spent his life
playing back whispers.

On the Corner

A vocal line
somewhere between bebop
and choir practice,

street music
loud enough to cut
through traffic

even when no more
substantial
than a melting icicle.

That was the sound
made it all seem part
of the same thing,

despite all crumbling
ill-matched evidence
to the contrary: the colors

blurred after the rain,
the rusted springs dangling
without support,

tossed beyond hope
of an approving
scavenger.

Saturday Night

Puccini and John Wayne,
side by side,
the one with a cigarette
dangling from the corner
of his mouth, the other

leaning pensive
on his horse's saddle,
stare sidewise
at Lady Murasaki, who
bent toward her writing table

glances up suddenly
at the moon, and at Emily Dickinson
who looks straight ahead
neither at the moon
nor at anyone.

Perseus and Danaë Adrift

About some things it is best to be silent.
I went through being born all over again.
Until then there had been little but blur,
half-heard murmurs and half-seen bodies.

At the proper age for emerging into light and speech
I was thrust deeper into noise and darkness.
In the midst of wave-swirl my mother told stories.
That is why I am full of memorized circumstances

and know the origin of every place name
and the secret reason for each family disaster.
We were cut off from the idea
of ever landing anywhere. Her talk was shore.

For the Unworshipped Gods

When did they go
and where have they gone

naked and sagacious
clustering and hidden

quick to anger
and boundless in giving

who wandered cloaked
through autumn fenland

or ascended red-gray
in smoke glow

or poised on bare rock
wet and gleaming

the trees and rivers
soaked in their lust

strange ones sprawling promiscuous
in pockets of love and quarrel

by ancient laws condemned
to harshness of exile

the upper reaches of sky
still filled with their giggles

their stony sighs
issuing from what hole in the ground?

Allegory of Good Government

The injunction against speedboats
had not yet come into effect

or perhaps there was never to be
an injunction against speedboats.

The posters nailed to the wall
behind the cash register

had been there since before the war ended.
In a dream where nobody did anything

it was beautiful to walk
past noon trees to the small lake.

This is the life, someone said,
nobody tells you to do anything

except that with the damn speedboats
you cannot hear yourself think.

September 3rd

He cannot exist alone
who made of world

carries at least
that much around,

arranging itself
into sudden phrases –

"I find a position" (he asserts)
"in relation to something

that exists, no matter what,
without which I can't write" –

expounding a method
or philosophy of composition

to the young woman who administers
the oddly unfamiliar poetry program

of the equally blurry institution
where he has been invited to read,

except that, wouldn't you know,
he has forgotten his manuscript –

never mind, he'll read
some older ones, out of the books –

but he forgot them as well –
so has nothing

but the words
found in the mouth –

or not even –
they having already escaped

back into the world
they are made of

or that some element in them
made long since –

Senseless

Like getting hit
on the head
with a hammer
or stumbling
into a basin
of water,
that is how
this poem
got written.

It had no name
when it was born;
it had no point
when it was done;
it sang about itself to itself,
and the quicker it started
the slower
it was ended.

The Back Country

Who stole the lake?
The frightful bandits
with their hats full of feathers,
they stole the lake.

When did they steal it?
When the sun was covered
with a cloud full of needles,
it was then they stole it.

Who shall retrieve it?
The hatless harrier
creeping through the brambles,
he shall retrieve it.

A Yard at Daybreak

Catching a cadence
from the deep city
you find a window
to watch the dawn by.

The shapes are laid out
ready for day.

There's one like a jug,
another like a net,
another like a basket
to put cut flowers in.

Who can remember
who laid them out?

The shop is shuttered
and the yard so quiet
you can hear the noise
of shadows vanishing.

Silence

What ever is the use
of stopping time – of watching
as the second hand slows down
and with enormous relief
the world settles into itself –
apocalypse as hiccup – an instant ago
the planets raced in their orbits,
now any stray wisp
of reflected light is universe enough –
even as the noise roars in
of motorbikes on the highway
and wind in the half-built skyscrapers.

III

After Calderón

Prince Ferdinand Compares Flowers to Stars

Perhaps it was to speak for the stars
that these flowers came.
These which were joy and splendor
awaking at dawn of day
by evening will be a vain regret
asleep in the cold arms of night.
This glimmer that challenged Heaven,
iris bordered with gold and scarlet and snow,
will become an emblem of human life.
So much can happen in one day.
The roses woke at dawn to flower
and flowered to grow old,
womb and tomb in a single bud,
as happens to men.
In one day they were born and died.
A century, when it's gone, is like an hour.

Princess Fenix Compares Stars to Flowers

Those flashes of light, sparks
that from the sun's splendors
derive ominous portents,
live only long enough to mourn for.
They are flowers of the night. Their fires
although beautiful are transient.
If one day for the flowers is a century,
a single night for the stars is an age.
That fugitive springtime

forecasts all our good and all our evil.
It inscribes if for any of us
the sun will live or die.
What lifespan can a man hope for
or what mutability endure
that he does not receive from a star
that each night is born and dies?

(an exchange from *The Constant Prince*, 1629)

Program Notes for a Festival of Lost Films

La Machine à Penser (1903)

The hands have no control over what the eyes see.
The subject is strapped down and forced to look at stars
that rotate in millwheel patterns. They swell
and diminish and at moments explode. It looks like the universe
but it is all controlled by the mind. Without conscious will
he touches down on planets and by gestures tries to speak
with strangers. Blows are struck. He runs.
Losing his footing he finds himself tumbling head over heels
into the bottomless abyss of space. As he falls
he stares back at his body strapped to the apparatus,
calmly observing the figures on the screen.

La Mer Ancienne (1908)

The sea is topped with glitter. The foam
seems to come to life. In the darkness we see heads
poke out of the water. All the dead are coming back,
not all at once but from one scattered pocket
then another of the vast deep. Like flowers they pop up
or like hidden armies. These are the legions
of the drowned, permitted to show themselves
when no one is watching. So many that after a time
the ocean is invisible, there is nothing but this crowd
of skeletons dripping with brine,
draped in the costumes of a thousand city-states
and vanished expeditions. They reach toward one another
as if to join hands in a delirious round-dance
where they never touch. In vain lunges
they try to rise above the water
but are never quite clear of it. Then as if on signal
they sink together under the rim.
The full moon shines over the empty sea.

The Girl of the Lost Lake (1911)

A grizzled master of woodcraft
sometimes shows up in these parts,
emerging unannounced into clearings.
He tells visitors where game is.
But he cannot be relied on after dark.
Then the peculiar omens turn up,
the speared owl, the mummified hand,
the half-burnt map whose burnt part
would have shown how to get out of here.
That is why they call it the lost lake.
The girl sometimes sighted crossing the water
by canoe, and who no sooner sets foot
on shore than she disappears among trees,
is said to be the second-sighted guardian
of what even the old man has forgotten.
This all happened because of an inheritance that was stolen.

On the Trail of Hate (1912)

They take rocks for cover in that country.
From a high dead point
they survey the roads of the region.
They wait until the sun has beaten into torpor
the approaching wagon train
and then descend in fury,
half hidden by the dust they stir up.
This is only one instance
of their empire of massacre and extortion.
They walk in disguise on plank roads
and write names in ledgers.
A peculiar emblem, like a star dripping blood,
is affixed to certain names.
People spy through knotholes.
Outriders are observed fleeing and do not get far.
It is difficult to make any headway
in a country so clotted with secret observation posts
and where any cellar or stable
may harbor an arsenal of destructive weaponry.
The most ordinary roads are dangerous,
whether or not there is anywhere to hide.

The Forbidden Path (1914)

In the secret kingdom a shadow screams.
Under the idol there is a cave entrance
and in the cave there is a trail
and at the end of the trail there is a bracelet,
the "opal bracelet" of which it was written
that the wearer of it shall come suddenly
upon a moss-covered idol. Under the idol
there is a cave entrance. The scream never ends.

The Death Studio (1915)

In this warren of cubbies are ivory pen-holders,
oval photographic portraits, safe-boxes
holding gems and testaments, an Asian mask,
a sword hung over the mantel, bookshelves rickety
from the stained volumes piled on them.
And on the floor an engagement ring
belonging to the person who like so many before
was seen entering but never seen to leave.
With its layers of seams and false fronts
it has become the repository
of absence. Squadrons of investigators
camp out here and find nothing
except what they were not looking for.
In such fashion the empty room
grows more crowded by the day.

Shadows of Sin (1920)

Here everything seems to have been changed
into cloth or flesh or flame or water
or burnished metal. One can no longer tell the difference.
There is a waving as of giant palm fronds.
They are mirrored by equally immense fans
woven of feathers. The camera need not even move
because whatever it shows is in rippling motion.
Impossible to see just where the ripples are going.
This does not last long. Everywhere else is made out of rock.

Her Double Life (1921)

This one puts wigs on and off,
makes herself up to be unrecognizable after church,
disappears into obliquely angled entrances
on tortuously narrow side streets. One day
somebody will meet her in the wrong neighborhood,
it's always almost happening. In the interim
her life is this carving out of shortcuts back and forth
between distinctively different lighting schemes,
either everything is bathed in bare cold light
with no hidden corners or else fine mist and flickers
play around the edges of bodies as they move.
The places where the lamps are always burning
never even see the places where the sun beams
on washing lines and muddy vegetable gardens.

The Desert Flower (1923)

Whitened almost past seeing,
her childhood in vanished tents.
A blossom known only by the song scheme
in which it served as rhyme.
Across trackless distances
the name was preserved by a structural device
traditional among nomads.
Even in the far-off city by the ocean
there was one who recognized the phrase
for which her name provided
the only rhyme possible. Then he understood
why he was brought here and instructed
to remain obediently in the courtyard
for what seemed eternity. And then he saw
an oasis in the empty sky above his head.
With mad certainty he rushed into the desert.

La Perla di Hawaii (1925)

Movie stars and financiers
regularly disembark on these shores
and never want to leave again.
Most depart but a few stay.
One of those will be changed forever
by an encounter with the young woman
they call "la perla di Hawaii."

Yûrei no ryôkan [The Inn of Ghosts] (1926)

How can the camera photograph
wind in darkness? By registering
what gets blacked out. The curtain
knocks over the lamp. The flare
as the light fails
resembles the character for "eye."
The fireflies in the garden of the inn
resemble a thousand floating eyes.

The Third Eye (1927)

In an otherwise empty room
a person kills another person.
The body is disposed of
and the room is as empty as before.
No one can ever know what happened.
But all the same there was a witness.
The room is not a real room
but a set in a film studio.
A camera had been left running.
When the investigators develop the film
they see everything. They project the film
for the murderer, who goes mad.
Afterwards the reel is formally burned
to avoid scandal.

The Crystal Prism (1928)

Strangers pass in and out of dozens of entrances,
invisible because made of glass. What seems air
is labyrinth. Two persons who appear to stand
next to each other are separated by a wall. Yet those
who enter there know their way among the turns,
can trace the curves and descents almost blindly
like waterdrops moving by capillary action.
It is only the intruder anxious to steal their secrets
who mistakes the trap for a passageway.
Multiplied by windows upon windows
he cannot distinguish reflections from apertures.
Utterly alone on an open plain
with no obstacles or markings anywhere near him
he discovers himself locked up like a prisoner.

New York Harbor (1929)

The harbor
is magic
in the moonbeams.
On a bench
the two of them
bide.
A barge
slides by
toward deep darkness,
how cold
the water
slaps in its wake.
On a bench
a kiss
or a cigarette
lights up the city
populated
only by two.

The Coast of Skeletons (1930)

The news was late
getting back from the beach
poisoned by alcohol.
Forbidden trade agreements
brought sails
into the folded harbor.
The dead pearl diver
walks on the reef.
"Ukulele of broken dreams"
they sang stomping
to the blind man's accordion.
Just plain exhausted
was what they were
from taking so many photos of foam.

Jungle

for Robert Kelly

"There are some events of which each circumstance
seems to be graven on the memory in such fashion
that we cannot forget it" (H. Rider Haggard)

Out of the book
comes fiery
flower,
nude magic veiled
by cave smoke. In an hour
outside of time
she reveals
herself and disappears
into herself.
The novel is held open
all night
until it dissolves.
The years are rain
in which a door
is always being opened
just past midnight
and a dying man
is pressing
a yellowed map
into the hand
of an uncomprehending stranger.
The page is the door.
The page is the drawer
where the recipient hides it
for another twenty years.
The words fuse

into canopies of feathers,
long narrow stretches
of masonry
that by torchlight
reveal archaic tracings
their priests made
in which from harbors
(now sunken)
winged boats fly
toward outer settlements.
This is beauty.
This is dread.
This is the dead.
Here everything
comes back to life
in the dark
in the dance of forms
that holds the captives rapt
until dawn erases it.
An underground world
where what is broken
is bright.
Everything buried
blossoms
as indigo cloud
or flame-colored signal
flickering
on rock wall.
Stayed up all night
having found the secret
of what never went away.
A truth not imagined
but imagining.
This dead mouth
is going to keep talking

even when the book is closed,
even when no reader
will ever
open it again.

Kleist

The sun operates
by law. Men
grow up wild under it.
Speech lifts off
light as sparrows
from a bush. The walls
between syllables
are mountainous.
Having always already
arrived even before
getting there he has time
to arrange his silence
into heraldic patterns.
The waves wash
plague coasts clean
of travelers' bones.
Where marauders
once mourned
their lost freedom
the yacht club flags
flap yellow.
A plume of smoke
plays on the water
like an edict.
He grabs what gleam
he can from the spark
where one facet of plating
shears hard against another.

The Woman Who Loved Mist

The flagstones are wet
as if it had rained
all day but there has been
no rain any day
except for gold
and red leaves falling
in continuous shower
to lie in heaps
until the morning
when a fine frost
coats the surface
of each fallen leaf
and by evening
a mist glistens
in the bare branches
that next day
has thickened
and spread so that
when she walks
to the edge of the lake
there is no lake

The Chimes

1
The nature of time

Is to dissolve
Into reverberations

The character of dusk
Is to proclaim them

2
I am once again
Where I never was before

In a town unknown to me
Even when I lived here

3
They sound like
Shivers of light
Clashing

Like the sound of glass
As it shatters
Into shadows of shadows

4
They sound like
The inmost lock

Springing
The subtlest catch
Coming loose

5
Or a bundle of keys
Dropped on a metallic sky

6
Where we are walking
Is always somewhere else
Already gone

7
Crosscut saw
Sliding sideways through time

8
In the same place
And the same hour

A different place
And a different hour

Unending coincidence
Of separations

A walk
Through frosty air

9
Disconnected sky
Seen from inside itself

10
In which is blue glow
Flame color
Not seen but heard
Not heard but

Apart from

11
Jars the street

Or as when
Pressing one surface on another

The registration is off

12
The body finds a way
To the contours
Of what was ditched

And in the wrong year
Walks home
Past unidentifiable archways

Insomnia

1
All at once
the carnival is canceled,
a stalker escapes from a clinic,
three people are dead in a trailer park,
whales are stressed by ship noise,
a black hole eats asteroids.

2
Home movies
of a world that no longer exists.

The twig looked like a dead lizard.

But what would a lizard have been doing
on Madison Avenue in late October?

3
Witness of the unwritten.

Limestone bluff
with nobody looking at it.

4
The main part of the hulk
went under so long after
the weight shifted below decks

that through all that interval
it seemed more than ever
buoyantly afloat.

5
Someone had invented
a new kind of camera movement

in which the camera fails
to keep up with what it tracks,

arriving just as the fugitive
has left the frame

to photograph
trampled grass.

6
In the present
I try to recreate a present

I saw in the past
only obliquely

being absorbed in a past
that looked just like a future

to be spent so deeply rapt
in the study of the past

that by the time the future came
I had gone back the other way.

7

I cannot possibly
mistake my unvoiced
imitation of your voice,
myself repeating to myself
a phrase you spoke,

for the voice itself
hovering by some means
at the edge of silence,
not whole enough
to speak a word

but trembling underneath,
the residue of breath
almost audible, here
where you are, barely,
and nowhere else.

8
Not knowing who
or what we are
we at least know when.

9
A madman in the subway
tosses out disjoined words
the way an insomniac tries
to make himself sleepy

by free association,
keeping the words
as far apart as possible
so he can drift off
into the gaps between meanings.

10
If mind found a place
of contained fire

warded from
wind and rain

it might delve
in dry darkness

to its own root
so calm as almost to let go.

11
He cannot tell the truth
because the truth is not in him.

He wasn't present
when he did the things
there are no words for.

12
It doesn't know
how it got here

but it does know
how odd it is.

13
"Most of the things
a movie can say
it can say in one frame."

By authority of dream.

14
Mind both last drug
and final addict

hooked
on its own windings

watches movies itself wove
out of empty night.

15
Not even a line from a poem,
the ruined memory of a line

scanned forty years before
on paper whose grain

my fingers
can still feel.

16
This cup,

how much
can it hold.

Hardly a drop.

17
In the book where
another man's life was written

my life was written.
A book made of dark water

spilling
over its own edges.

18
Blurred scroll
of a river life

adjacent to whatever
the neighbors are cooking.

Anything you touch
is alive.

Anything anyone
touches

is dangerously
alive.

19
Some from the air
have taken poison.

Their eyes
beyond rescue,

all the history
of their fear

laid out
like an all-night game of Risk.

20
"Mother,
let me in—"

Graveyard
of living books

where black words
glisten.

The light
of another sun

ground up
into black powder.

21
They live on boats.

Canal.
Ancient flowering bridge.

The young girls
are scented with lilac.

Alive. Not exactly alive.

More alive
than what is not here.

22
A book
that can be read

only where there is
no light,

whose lines are made
not of sunlight

but what
sunlight becomes,

by what
comes of it.

The Birds

the mornings
are now part of me

when the clarity
of being awake all night

tapered off
into the clarity of dawn

the incredible process
of bodies becoming visible

no need of electric light
no need of night or sleep

at those times thought was difficult
if it can be called thought

a cross between groping
and being flooded

something like being in love
without an object of love

nothing but a world
made real by touching it

made whole by being
cracked open

in time to the birds
in the unseen garden

here now here now cheep
here now cheep

kick it keep it
kick it keep it

hither hither whence
hither whence

aweep aweep aweep
aweep aweep